Don't Go Fishing Without A Hook

Step-by-step Premarital Guide

Breckney G. Shaw

ISBN: 979-8-9917280-4-1

Table of Contents

Introduction

Decades ago, there was a famous singer and songwriter, Al Green, who released a hit recording of his song entitled "Tired of Being Alone." The lyrics remind us of how a person can come to a point in their life where they are literally tired of being alone. Grocery shopping, for one, gets old, and being a member of a wedding party is flattering, but after the celebration is over, you'll return to your home alone. There comes a time when you are ready to settle down with someone you can love dearly and have them love you in the same way. Scripture tells us after God created Adam, He said, "It is not good for the man to be alone; I will make him a helper suitable for him." This statement has implications for both men and women. After God removed a rib from Adam and designed from Adam's rib a woman, God brought her to him to be his suitable counterpart. What happened in Genesis chapter two fulfills God's plan in Genesis chapter one. God said, "Let us make man in our own image, and in our likeness, male and female, he created them" (Genesis 1:17). Human beings are social beings by design. It is not normal for a person to want to live in isolation away from family and friends. As humans mature and move from adolescence to adulthood, the single status box remains with them until they marry.

However, marriage may not be for everyone. There are several reasons why some adults prefer a single life over a married life. Some are single because they haven't found the right person to marry. Others have the gift of being single and have no desire to marry. Then there is the group who are single again after divorce, the death of a spouse, or a breakup. Another reason can be found in an interesting article in Psychology Today by Fredric Neuman, MD, exploring the question, "Why can't some people find anyone to marry? However, once a person becomes aware that they no longer desire to be alone and no longer desire to pursue another girlfriend or boyfriend relationship, they are ready to search for a spouse.

Years ago, after finding my potential spouse, I brought her to meet my parents. After meeting my parents, I took her to visit my grandparents, whom we affectionately call Mom and Pop. They were happily married for over 60 years and had 12 children. My siblings and I were fortunate to live with them during our early years. I remember our bedroom was next to theirs and that they talked a lot, particularly at night, in their bed. I also recalled they laughed a lot and worked together as a team. One of the things they did well was to know the character of anyone we brought around them. So, I wanted to get their feedback and impression of her before going any further in the relationship. The visit seemed to have gone well.

Before my girlfriend and I left their home, my grandfather said to me, "**Son, don't go fishing without a hook**." I was perplexed by the statement, but I didn't ask what he meant by it. After several months, the riddle bothered me because I didn't understand what he meant. So, I finally decided to think about what he was saying. Then I asked myself, why would anyone go fishing without a hook? You don't plan to catch fish if you do not have a hook. You are either wasting your time or pretending to fish. So my interpretation of my grandfather's riddle is: **Don't waste her time if you are not serious about marrying her.** Later on, I married her. We have been happily married for 37 years and counting.

Some may wonder how do you find that special someone to marry. Given the high divorce rate, many have a fearful or pessimistic view of marriage. Being a fun-loving couple early in the marriage doesn't mean divorce is out of the picture in the future. Sometimes, people change over time and morph into different people who no longer adhere to "till death do us part." On the other hand, from my experience and that of several friends, we know it is possible to have a harmonious marriage if you are patient with the process and **experience true love with the right person**. When your love for each other is mutually unconditional, it can last till death or the Rapture brings it to an end. If you decide to pursue a spouse, I recommend you do it in a manner **that does not waste time**. Searching for a spouse does not mean you need to be in a hurry to marry, but you do need to be intentional.

The **purpose of this book** is to give you a strategy and process to help you **manage your time and vet people** so that you can make the wisest choice possible. The term vet means to *evaluate for possible approval or acceptance*. Can I guarantee you will have a divorce-proof marriage? No, that will be up to the two people involved in the marriage. There are several things that can lead to divorce. However, theologically, Jesus gives us insight into the root cause of divorce.

Jesus said, "Because of your hardness of heart, Moses permitted you to divorce your wives, but from the beginning, it has not been this way. Marriage is made by God's design, but divorce is not designed by God. He permits it, but it has painful and sometimes harmful consequences.

The phrase hardness of heart comes from the Greek word *sklerokardia*, which refers to stubborn or completely unyielding and unfeelingness. *Kardia* is the Greek word for heart and refers to the inner man's intellect, will, and emotion. When someone has a hard heart, *intellectually*, they know what they should do but refuse to acknowledge what they know is right. When someone has a hard heart, *volitionally*, they can choose to do what is right but refuse to choose to do the right thing. Lastly, when someone has a hard heart, *emotionally*, they can feel what the right thing is and ignore or suppress what they feel is the right thing to do.

Therefore, the marriage is over when one or both parties reach this point. So, as you go through this book, invest your time wisely as you discover that person who has a heart for you and you for them.

Step 1
Preparation for the Venture

Love yourself before you can love someone else

Before you go searching for your true love, you need to know whether you love yourself or not. If you don't love yourself, how will you truly love someone else? Unfortunately, people who do not love themselves can end up neglecting themselves or hurting themselves. Self-neglect can have negative consequences. So, care enough about yourself to consider loving yourself.

The Bible is a great source of wisdom and answers to everyday issues. As it relates to love, Jesus teaches us that the main object of our love is God. Loving God involves an intellectual, volitional, emotional encounter and interaction with God, your creator. When people embrace the reality of a true and living God, they will have further access to Him through faith in His Son Jesus, prayer, meditation, His written word, and the Holy Spirit. When we practice loving God, it will prepare us to love ourselves and our neighbor. Being able to love your neighbor properly is predicated on your ability to love yourself. However, you can't genuinely love yourself if you don't love God. When you can display your love for God, you will also have insight into how good He is. The God of the Bible is so good and loves you so much that He gave His only Son, Jesus Christ, to die in your place and give you an eternal covenant of forgiveness. As one who is forgiven by God, you are granted eternal access to Him and His kingdom. God only wants the best for you. God does not abandon you when you mess up, but He will rescue you and restore you if you value your relationship with Him.

Once you think about who God is and what he has done for you, it should put a smile on your face and gratitude in your heart. This type of insight helps you acknowledge that God is merciful and kind, forgiving, and willing to adopt you and make you a part of His divine royal family. Keep in mind that we are made in the image of God. Each of us is an original. Originals are worth more than copies. When you respect yourself, love yourself, and recognize your healthy uniqueness, it makes you a prize, not a consolation prize. No one can beat you at being you.

Unfortunately, some people do not see themselves as attractive or worthy of divine love and struggle to love themselves. They begin to engage in self-hatred and destructive behavior and have low self-esteem and feelings of depression. Many often turn to drugs, alcohol, and sex to battle depression stemming from loneliness. Often, many singles do not know how to cope with the grief of loneliness. The excessive use of drugs and alcohol abuse does not resolve the problem.

They can also have a distorted self-image based on shame and negative self-talk. Negative self-talk tends to lead to negative interpretation, which leads to ill feelings and a negative attitude or behavior toward yourself and others.

When you love God, you can love yourself. When you love yourself, you will carry yourself differently. Recognizing your worth as a child of God makes you feel better about yourself. Once you accept yourself and realize God values you, you can truly love yourself because God loves you. If you love yourself, you can love your neighbor.

To help us understand loving our neighbor, Jesus tells the story of the good Samaritan to explain who a neighbor is. Interestingly, if you did everything the good Samaritan did for the stranger (neighbor) who was left half dead on Jericho Road, you could find applications for loving yourself.

Observe first of all: When the Samaritan saw the wounded man on the road in terrible shape, he didn't ignore what he saw; He attended to the need. **If you applied this truth to yourself, you would** have compassion for yourself when it comes to dealing with personal wounds. **Secondly**, if you have a problem you can't fix alone, **seek treatment to help** you get well. **Thirdly**, the Samaritan spent money on the man's care. **Consider investing in your self-care**. Practicing self-care is a part of self-love.

Therefore, loving yourself and others becomes possible when you are intentional about loving God and worshipping Him. The scripture says children of God are to love Him with all their heart and with all their soul and with all their strength and with all their mind.

Know yourself

Next, in the preparation stage, you need to know yourself; you need to know what you like and dislike. You need to know if you are patient or impulsive. Are you responsible or irresponsible? Do you have anger issues or untreated past trauma? Have you ever been told you are mean-spirited or selfish? You need to know your anger triggers and what makes you happy or sad. Do you struggle with impulse control disorders, depression, anxiety, or narcissistic personality disorder? Do you struggle with various mental or physical health issues that have gone untreated? Do you have attachment issues that have negatively impacted previous relationships? If you are unsure about any of the above, you may want to schedule an appointment with a counselor or therapist to help you work through your issues.

Know your motivation for pursuing a spouse

As you begin this journey, do you know why you want a spouse? Are you pursuing a spouse because you want someone to keep you company, to have regular sex with, or someone to help you buy a house or go on vacation with? Or are you looking for someone to keep you warm at night, or have children with, or to marry someone who is your best friend and who you want to spend the rest of your life with? In your search for a spouse, make sure you both have the right motivations.

As you begin your search for a potential spouse, you must be willing to cognitively transition from "**A Me mindset**" to "**A We mindset**". Depending on your age and personality, you may struggle to make this adjustment, particularly if you believe you are set in your ways. In order to have marital harmony, you have to be considerate of the other person. Being flexible, empathic, and understanding of what a person needs in different stages of life is beneficial. For instance, some single guys may not realize the sense of urgency a woman may have in her childbearing years. Many men do not realize younger women may be looking at their biological clock and wanting to have children. Some couples want biological kids, and others want to adopt children. Some single women may not realize that if a man is not mature and ready for marriage, he **will not** make the best choice for a husband. There is a scripture that says two can't walk together unless they agree.

Make sure you are on the same page about what you want to accomplish with your potential spouse. Explore whether you have the same expectations or different ones. Do you both want a nice wedding, picket fence, house, children, etc., or something else? Having different objectives can lead to multiple problems and drama. Look for common ground and be clear on what **your deal-**

breakers are. *Deal breakers are your non-negotiables or zero-tolerance issues.*

Protect yourself

After doing a reasonable amount of work on yourself, be intentional about setting a few ***essential boundaries*** in your intimate partner relationship.

> *An intimate partner is a close personal relationship between individuals who identify as a couple that is characterized by some of the following dimensions: emotional connection, regular contact, and ongoing physical contact that need not be sexual, as defined by IGI Global Publishing House.*

The two boundaries I will mention are essential keys to your success. However, you will need to rethink the way you will conduct future relationships moving forward. You may be familiar with this saying, often credited to Albert Einstein, which is that *"insanity is doing the same thing over and over again and expecting different results."* From a Cognitive Behavioral Therapy perspective, if a person can change the way they think, they can change the way they behave. Nonetheless, these boundaries may be contrary to our present cultural norms, but they will, more often than not, yield better results.

The two boundaries are: **1. Practice Non-exclusivity in your intimate partner relationship. 2. Practice Abstinence** in the development of your intimate partner relationship. *Nonexclusive* means you choose **not** to be in a committed relationship ***before you are engaged or married***. *Non-exclusivity* protects your single status. It provides a safety net to help protect your heart from heartbreak and reduce needless drama from toxic people. **Setting a Nonexclusive boundary** can be done by learning to communicate this concept on the first date by saying: ***"I do not want to be in an exclusive relationship until I am engaged to be married."***

One of the pitfalls of modern-day dating is to allow oneself to enter into an *exclusive relationship* with a **stranger** you are attracted to or hooked up with, hoping it works out. ***An exclusive relationship is one where the boyfriend and girlfriend operate as a married couple.*** You are doing everything that married people do without a license. You do not allow each other the freedom to talk to or date anyone else. Usually, in this type of relationship, there is a lot of jealousy, insecurity, manipulation, and emotional ups and downs. These are very challenging issues for someone who is not ***engaged or married.***

Another drawback of being in an ***exclusive relationship, unmarried or unengaged***, is that of taking yourself off the market too soon. This is not your best move. ***It is actually to your disadvantage*** to give up your ***autonomy*** by deciding ***prematurely*** to be in an exclusive intimate partner relationship ***with a stranger***. Have you considered how risky it is to commit yourself to a stranger you truly do not know? You do not know who they are when they are not trying to impress you. You do not know how many people they may have been sexually active with before meeting you. If you settle too soon, you may give someone **the best years of your life** before you realize **it was a mistake.** If this is your story, this book is what you need to *reboot, start over, and create a new beginning.*

A word of caution

Resist giving up your autonomy and single status to operate as a married or engaged person without knowing whom you are choosing. You may think it is love, but it could be lust. John Gottman reports that lust can last up to 2 years. The problem with lust is that it may feel like love, but in the long run, it does not have what unconditional love provides. *Unconditional love* is loving someone as they are. Too many people make the mistake of believing they can *change* the person into becoming who they want them to be. When that fails, they become more dissatisfied and are ready to abandon the relationship. But unconditional love has no conditions. It includes **acceptance** of the person as they are. A better term to describe what happens in an intimate partner relationship is *passion verses lust.* Having passion is not a bad thing. However, the relationship is healthier if it stands on more than passion. It will be very difficult for couples to be drawn toward each other without passion. Gottman declares love has three components*: passion, trust, and commitment.* Without all three, you do not have genuine love.

Understanding the four types of Love

The Greeks have four words for expressing love: **Philia**, love between close friends or brothers; **Eros**, sensual or romantic love; **Storge**, love between family members; and **Agape**, unconditional, sacrificial love. In a marriage, you will experience all four as you go through the various stages of life. But the apostle Paul, one of the great writers of scripture, gives us one of the best descriptions of *agape love* as he writes the following:

[4] Love is patient, love is kind, it is not jealous; love does not brag, it is not arrogant. [5] It does not act disgracefully, it does not seek its own *benefit*; it is not provoked, does not keep an account of a wrong *suffered,* [6] it does not rejoice in unrighteousness but rejoices with the truth; [7] it [a]keeps every confidence, it believes all things, hopes all things, endures all things(1 Corinthians 13:4-7). Love never fails.

Don't let sex cloud your judgment

In the *Eros* type of love, the feelings of passion can be so overwhelming and tempting to the point one may stop resisting and allow sexual intercourse into the relationship too soon. Engaging in sexual intercourse early in the development of the relationship can cloud your judgment and your ability to think about what type of person you are getting involved with because of how the sex feels. Good sex is great, but it can impair your reasoning ability when vetting a life partner. Good sex for others can seal the deal.

Nevertheless, a lot of singles have enjoyed good sex, but it didn't necessarily get them a good husband or wife. Don't let your impulsivity set you up for possible failure. Also, you may want to watch Tyler Perry's movie *Temptation: Confessions of a Marriage Counselor* before falling for having sex with a stranger. Some people are Trojan horses. They may look good on the outside, fit, fine, beautiful, or handsome, but they have something you really don't want. In the United States, hundreds of thousands of people who have HIV or other STDs do not get tested, and it doesn't matter your sexual orientation. You may want to do some homework before you get too infatuated with new relationships. However, there are ways to get tested anonymously or privately to ensure your safety. Make sure you know the sexual health of your intimate partner as well. Exchange test results and have peace of mind if abstinence is not your path. It is better to be safe than sorry. Hopefully, you can see why character is important.

Don't let your relationships manage you

As we move along, rethink how you do relationships by becoming ***active*** rather than ***passive*** in your management style. This is a powerful concept to adhere to. Perhaps in the past, you didn't know how to be in control of your life and maintain your ***autonomy*** as a single person. Your past relationship management style may have been influenced purely by feelings and the visual aesthetics of a person's anatomical makeup. Unfortunately, this approach may get you caught in a riptide. This means you are carried away by feelings and fantasy before you stop and realize you are deeply involved in a toxic relationship.

Maintain your boundaries to filter out people who are trying to enter your space for the wrong reasons. Resist the temptation to **take yourself off the singles market prematurely**, fearing you may lose an opportunity with this new person. Do not allow negative self-talk, negative interpretations, or low self-esteem to make you fearful, insecure, and impatient. Instead, allow yourself time to meet others and form quality relationships while keeping your single status in **non-exclusive relationships**.

For *example*, if you could pick four cars of your choice to vet and money was not an object, which one would be your final choice? How would you know which car you liked the best? You would not know the answer to that question without having experienced each car. Over time, you will discover that some of the cars may be high maintenance, and others are nothing but trouble even though they look good. Then there is the car that is reliable, comfortable, luxurious, and only requires reasonable periodic maintenance. However, if you start out committed to only one car that you do not know much about, you can, in many cases, waste time and invest in a bad choice. Unfortunately you may be stuck with it.

Therefore, I recommend giving yourself time to go through the stages of selecting a mate without all the usual collateral damage such as heartbreak, unwanted pregnancy, STD, and being in a relationship with a bad character who does not share your values. It takes **patience** and **a plan** to find a lifetime mate while enjoying the experience of searching without drama. Implementing this **new management style** allows you to *take control* of the process shared in the following stages.

Step 2
Dating Stage 1

The goal is to find up to four highly valued friends

These days, finding new friends is difficult, even if you show yourself to be friendly. It is also hard to find friends if you do not know how to search for friends. But how do you begin looking for intimate partner friendships?

One way to jump-start your search is to look in the area of your passions and personal interests (e.g., sports, hobbies, activities, clubs, church, malls, shows, etc.). Meeting new people through an introduction from close friends, relatives, and associates is usually an easier way to do so. If you are spiritual, pray and ask God to send a spouse that meets the biblical standard and your standard. Use this standard to avoid the wolf in sheep's clothing. Once you find a prospective new friend, arrange an initial meeting, sometimes called a ***date***.

Consider the dating process, like reviewing job applications to see who gets the in-person interview. Once the stranger is in front of you in person, vet them to decide if you would consider a second date. If they are open to it, express your desire for a second date. You do this to gather more information and see if the mutual attraction continues. This will determine if they get moved to the potential friend zone (PFZ) or to the drop zone (DZ). You will do this vetting at least 3 to 4 times. Don't be tempted to be the one friend at a time person. Remember the goal is to have up to four quality friends available to you that you are not in an exclusive relationship with.

As you search for new quality friendships, you may not be aware of this, but the *Dating Stage* can be one of the most deceptive and stressful phases for those pursuing an intimate partner relationship. **Do not forget,** you are getting to know a stranger. In the dating stage, most people are on their best behavior. Gary Chapman's work with couples reveals truths about how people understand love. When singles are dating, they can mysteriously engage in various love languages. Often, they are unaware these languages are having a positive effect during their interaction with each other.

As mentioned earlier, people are usually on their best behavior on the first date. They tend to connect using physical touch, words of affirmation, quality time, acts of service, and gift-giving. Each love language positively affects how one responds to the stranger they are getting to know. In this dating experience, you may feel good because you are responding to these various touch points. However, this is where the first meeting can be deceptive because although it feels good, you still do not know who this person is *when they are not trying to impress you*. You do not even know their true character, and they do not know your true character.

Dating can be more challenging for introverts

Dating can be more challenging for introverts than for extroverts. **Introverts** gain energy by being away from people, while **extroverts**, on the other hand, gain energy from being with people. Introverts may experience social anxiety because they are not comfortable being assertive with strangers. Extraverts are more comfortable meeting new people and can be the life of the party. Another personality type is **ambiverts;** they tend to be natural introverts who can become extroverts. However, they would rather be away from people when they can because being around people for a long period of time tends to be draining. So, knowing your personality type can help you make the adjustments or disclosures you need to make if you want to make new friends.

Hindrances to making new friends

When you are trying to make new friends, a lack of confidence or coming across as desperate is not attractive to those you are trying to attract. Making negative statements or being rude is also not attractive. Inappropriate, aggressive, threatening behavior toward others is a turnoff. Poor oral or body hygiene can be repulsive. People who are too talkative or poor listeners can be annoying. Lastly, spending a lot of time talking about oneself or past failed relationships can also be a turnoff.

Focus on the goal of dating

The primary motivation for dating is to make new friends that could give you viable choices for a potential spouse. Unfortunately, some *demonize* the term **friendship when used in reference to people of the opposite sex as being boring or unwanted.** In other words, there is no chance for romance. True **friendship** is a relationship not to be taken lightly. Jesus said, " Greater love has no man than this, and he would lay down his life for his friends." Friends are important and extremely valuable. In a true friendship, there is the desire to guard relational harmony.

- True friends don't hurt each other.
- They don't try to control each other.
- True friends will not betray each other.
- They don't disrespect each other.
- True friends love each other.
- They trust each other.
- They are honest with each other.
- True friends will protect each other.
- They will love each other.
- True friends will tell each other the truth.
- They laugh with each other.
- True friends have fun and enjoy being with each other.

So why would you choose a spouse who is not a true friend?

You need a viable plan for making quality friends

Having a good plan when fishing for quality intimate partner friendships is not just helpful; it's essential. When it comes to attraction, your senses are engaged, particularly your sense of **sight** and **smell**. With a well-thought-out plan, you can navigate the dating world with confidence and purpose.

The first part of your plan needs to be your *external presentation.* It should include grooming, hygiene, physical fitness, and a nice wardrobe. What you see and smell matters. The second part of the plan is to reveal your inner self. Display your internal qualities, such as integrity, consideration, a positive thought process, flexibility within reason, and patience.

Good spiritual health can help the relationship go deeper. Do you have a moral compass or a sense of right and wrong? Conflict and challenges can arise within the relationship when people are not on the same page spiritually. Spiritual people connect with the inner being of others. They are compassionate and empathic. They can see beyond the externals and connect with the person's soul as they listen to them, walk with them, and speak to them.

As a reminder, "Decide to manage your relationships. Do not let your relationships manage you." You can put this strategy to work by deciding upfront to set two key boundaries to help you manage your relationships:

1. **Remain in a non-exclusive relationship until engagement or marriage.**

2. **Resist having sex early in the development of the relationship.**

You may ask, **why set these boundaries**? Setting these boundaries ensures that strangers do not invade your space unvetted. Boundaries exist to keep you and the other person safe. Also, you want to maintain your autonomy as you develop relationships with new people. Having *self-determination* gives you the freedom to be acquainted with whomever you choose without feeling restricted or bound to someone else as you search for quality friendships and make spontaneous decisions.

Next, one may ask **why abstinence**. The answer is **sex may cloud your judgment** and make it psychologically and biologically challenging to make a rational decision while vetting the person you are getting to know. When you allow *sex early* in the relationship with **a stranger** you barely know, it could cause emotional attachment issues. When you engage in sexual intercourse, a plethora of hormones are released. For instance, oxytocin, the bonding hormone, is released in your brain. This hormone can make it difficult to leave someone you do not like. During sexual intercourse, happy hormones like *dopamine and serotonin* are also at work. Something you may not be aware of is the brain activity of hormone release that could in a negative way create the behavior of an addict. This is only good if you have found the right match. Otherwise, you could find yourself wanting more sex to feel satisfied, not realizing you feel good not because of the relationship only but the sex and sometimes both.

Some people enter long-term relationships because of the sex, but they are not happy with their relationship. Notice that when the relationship goes bad, the sex gets cut off. To avoid repeating this classic mistake in intimate partner relationships, keep the abstinence boundary in place! I recognize some may say you don't know I have my needs. But how has that approach worked out for you?

Abstain from the use of drugs and alcohol

Although *abstinence* used here primarily refers to sex, let's not overlook the effects of drugs and alcohol. *Marijuana and alcohol* release *dopamine* into your system. Remember, dopamine is the happy hormone or feel-good hormone. So, if most of your interaction with your intimate partner involves drug use or excessive drinking, how will you know how you feel about the person when you are not under the influence? I recommend you curtail the use of substances until you truly get to know this stranger you are vetting before deciding to put them in the **PTZ**. If you cannot interact with your intimate partner without being under the influence, you will not make a good decision. However, if you struggle with alcohol and drug use, consider seeing a counselor or getting into a treatment program.

Another benefit of setting these boundaries is that it gives you a good idea of **who respects your boundaries and who does not.** Most boundary crossers tend to exercise *power and control* over their intimate partner. They are *manipulators and potential abusers*. It would be wise to nip this in the bud. Remember, you are single and autonomous (you make decisions for your life; you do not allow other people to decide for you). Do not allow a stranger to occupy a position of power and control in your life.

For example, boundary crossers may say they respect your desire not to be in a non-exclusive relationship, but when they see you with someone else in public, they may display a bad attitude. Those who don't respect boundaries could be the ones who blow up your phone or visit uninvited. This type of behavior warrants removal from the **PFZ** to the **DZ**.

Setting a nonexclusive boundary helps you remove undesirable people from the **PTZ** People with power and control issues have the potential to become abusive. Protect yourself from being caught in a domestic violence situation. *Domestic Violence emerges from a pattern of abusive behavior between people in a relationship where one person uses power and control over another*. One of the major problems with this type of entanglement is that the abused person often loves the abuser but hates the abuse. Avoid this quagmire as much as possible.

In abusive relationships, the abusive behavior or power and control can manifest itself in different types of abuse, such as:

physical, sexual, financial, religious, psychological, and emotional abuse. Do not tolerate abuse at all, whether single or married. Protect yourself from predators, stalkers, or whatever form abusers manifest themselves. Call the police, get a dog, talk to best friends, a counselor, take martial arts, etc. **Protect Yourself. Take Charge Legally!**

Guard your mental health

Managing your relationship in the dating stage of the intimate partner relationship can help you protect your physical and mental health. Vet people early to prevent getting into a bad relationship with anyone. Toxic relationships can cause one to feel trapped or codependent. These types of relationships can lead to anxiety, depression, drug addiction, low self-esteem, self-worth issues, suicidal ideation, or homicidal thoughts. If you struggle with any of these challenges due to a bad relationship, get help immediately.

Two types of Friendships

Remember, your goal is to acquire up to four quality intimate partners. They can be a combination of *plutonic friendships* or *romantic interest friendships*. Some people may wonder why keep both types of friends. You may have heard of stories of plutonic friends realizing over time that they know each other very well, trust each other, love each other, and don't want to spend the rest of their lives with anyone else. Let's call it a **Hallmark** moment. Then, romantic interest relationships can also blossom and bloom into lifetime relationships.

Evaluating your dating experience

Remember, in the **dating stage**, you are looking for people who respect your boundaries and whom you can move to the **PFZ**. So, what do you do after the first few dates? If you sense you have a good rapport with the person and it feels right, consider a second date in a public place with close friends or family who know your whereabouts.

If there is a lack of chemistry or interest after the second date, you may move this new person to the **DZ**. If this is your decision after careful consideration and it becomes clear you have lost interest, **affirm them as a person** and end any further development of the relationship unless things change. In the meantime, enjoy the privileges of not being in an *exclusive relationship* while the search continues.

Disciplines to keep in the dating stage

- Set boundaries of not being in an exclusive relationship

- Vet your dates to determine whether they will be moved from the PFZ to the DZ.

- Place potential friends who do not respect your boundaries into the drop zone.

- Look for people to put in the friend zone.

- No sex

Next, we move to stage 2, called the **courting stage.**

Step 3
Courting Stage 2

The goal is to narrow down your choice of whom to explore the possibility of marriage with

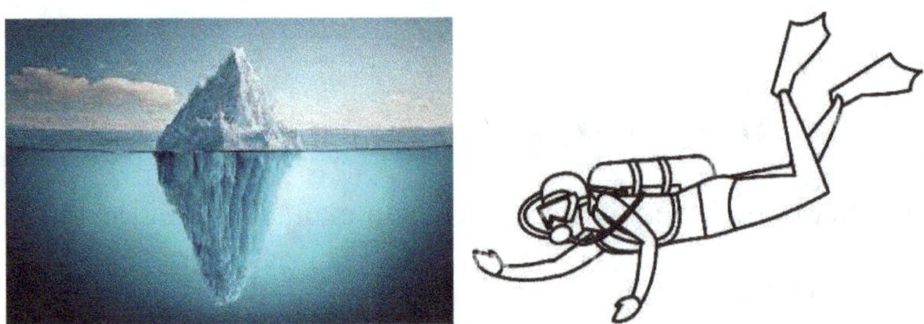

In the initial stages of an intimate partner relationship, what you see is not half of what you will get. It is like looking at the tip of an iceberg; only 10% is visible, and 90% is below the surface. When you enter this stage, know that it is time to figuratively go scuba diving and explore the depth of the person you have a romantic interest in.

During the **courting stage**, you narrow your choices to one particular person to select as a possible spouse. In this stage, you **expand** your knowledge of the person you have chosen to court. One way to embark upon this stage is to ask one of your friends with whom you are developing a close relationship, **"Is it okay to spend more time with you so I can get to know you better?"** Remember that it takes time and experience to acquire knowledge of someone you are forming a friendship with. As you take this journey of discovery, you want to keep healthy boundaries by mutual agreement. ***Non-exclusivity*** and ***abstinence*** remain in place.

Maintain healthy boundaries

You will still keep other friends at this stage while investing more time with the friend you are exploring as a potential spouse. Now, some may think that at this stage of the relationship, you can begin having sex. If you are serious about making your best decision, you will want to *hold off so that the sex does not cloud your judgment.* Some singles may rationalize that they cannot hold out that long. If you struggle with abstaining from sex before marriage, you may be experiencing *more Lust than Love,* or you have a *sex addiction.* Having a passion for someone is a healthy human trait. *The apostle Paul writes,* "But if they do not have self-control, let them marry; for it is better to marry than to burn *with passion.*" (1 Corinthians 7:9).

Please note: having sex should not be your only motivation for getting married. A husband or a wife is different than a boyfriend or girlfriend. A spouse is different from a side chick or a sugar daddy or simply a hookup.

Understand that Lust is a powerful sexual desire toward someone. For some people, once their lust is satisfied, they will be ready to move on. For others, they will stay for the next sexual encounter. If you are struggling with sex addiction, you will have excessive sexual thoughts, desires, urges, or behaviors that you cannot control and cause distress and harm to your relationships, finances, and other aspects of your life. Sexual addiction is also called hyper-sexuality, compulsive sexual behavior, and other names.

Unfortunately, people with sex addiction can also have problems with intimacy. They have trust issues and keep secrets about how they really feel and what they truly desire. They feel unsafe communicating their fears, fantasies, frustrations, etc. Therefore, they are not comfortable showing their true self. However, if this describes your situation, seek therapy to help you cope with your addiction or rule out other explanations.

Nevertheless, if you believe it is not addiction and you are struggling with self-control in the heat of passion wanting to have sex, I recommend you pump the brakes, walk away, and ask some serious questions before you risk baby mama drama or baby daddy drama.

Questions to ask yourself in advance

1. **Do I love them?**

2. **Do they love me?**

3. **Is this person my best friend?**

4. **Would I want this person to be the parent of my children?**

5. **Do we share the same family values?**

6. **Do they have an STD?**

7. **Are they self-sufficient?**

8. **Do they love Jesus?**

Please note that you are taking a significant risk to engage in sexual intercourse after saying **NO** to any of the questions above. The choice is yours, but I still recommend waiting and learning more about this new friend and stranger.

Having your two boundaries (non-exclusivity and abstinence) in place allows you to test the true character of your romantic interest. If sex is off the table, you will see who respects you and wants to get to know you better as a person.

Assessment tools for further vetting

While adhering to these critical boundaries, explore what you two have in common and where you are different by using assessment tools for further vetting. One tool you can use is the love language assessment from the online assessment found at *5Lovelanguanges.com*. A full report will require a small investment, but it is worth it. Once you both take the assessment, share the results with each other and keep the results in a safe place.

Note: If the person refuses to take the assessment, consider terminating the courtship and moving them from the Regular Friend Zone (**RFZ**) to the **DZ**.

Another assessment you will want to do is a *cultural values assessment.* Remember, you both come from different families of origin and maybe different ethnic groups or different countries. Since you are getting to know each other, you must understand what that person values and considers important in life. You can do a cultural assessment by

1. List your ten most important things (i.e., marriage, family, education, religion, etc.).

2. Use a blank sheet of paper with numbers from 1 to 10, and begin to list your values. The list is complete once you list at least 10.

If they refuse to do this exercise, consider ending the courtship and moving them to the **RFZ** or to the **DZ**. You might be thinking, "Wow, that seems harsh." However, people who resist reasonable requests could be hiding something, not connecting, or being stubborn. This type of behavior is a ***red flag*** and should not be ignored.

Meet your special friend's extended family

You will gain more insight upon meeting family and friends during the **courting stage** while staying in a ***nonexclusive relationship. Some people may struggle at this point because they fear losing this potential match.*** Remember, you are **not engaged**, and you are **not married**, so why act like you are married while you are still exploring? Another thing to be on the lookout for is ***the reluctance to introduce or bring you around family.*** This could be a ***red flag,*** or it could be their way of protecting you from toxic and sick family members. Perhaps your special love interest is the best member in a dysfunctional family system. Do not insist on meeting the family if they don't want you to. But consider ending the courtship and evaluating someone else if this is a ***deal breaker*** for you. On the other hand, once you have met their family and friends, it is time for introspection. Here are some questions to ask yourself:

1. **Are you experiencing a good rapport?**
2. **Does the family accept you as a potential spouse? The same is true when they meet your family.**
3. **Are you paying close attention to the feedback from your family and friends?**
4. **Have you considered the input from loving parents and close friends who love you and whom you love?**

Keep in mind that they see and sense things you do not see. I remember one of my best friends had been divorced twice. I told him not to propose to or marry anyone else until I vet them for him. I knew his basic type of woman would be pretty, fine, and well-groomed. So one day, I received a phone call from him, and he said, Man, I think I have found a keeper, but I want you to meet her. So, the three of us had dinner together, and I checked her out. I watched their interaction and asked some questions to check out her personality and motivation. By the end of the meal, I felt she was a good choice. They were only married for a short time, and he told me before he passed that of the three marriages, this was the happiest he had ever been. Subsequently, I strongly urge you to consider a close friend or valued family member's feedback and wise counsel. If the vibe is good, and you two enjoy each other's company, you can begin discussing the possibility of a future together in marriage.

The vibe can be the energy you feel from another person, whether good or bad. Sometimes, a couple can be in sync with the other person and breathe in similar ways. Sometimes, my wife and I notice we have the tendency to sigh and breathe at the same time. This is called **interbrain synchronization**. Scientific American has an interesting article related to this.

Next, invite them to go with you to **10 weeks of premarital counseling** to see if you should even seriously consider marriage.

However, if the person refuses to go to 10 weeks of premarital counseling, then consider whether to move them back to the **RFZ** or the **DZ**.

If they agree and want to move forward, I recommend working with a pastor, counselor, or psychotherapist who uses the **"Prepare-Enrich Assessment."** The beauty of using this assessment is that it is like having an MRI of your relationship together. It will reveal the trouble spots unseen or unrecognized in your relationship and show your strengths and growth areas. The results from the assessment will help you have essential discussions about communication, conflict resolution, financial management, sexual relationships, role expectations, family and friends, parenting, and spirituality.

After working through the growth areas for ten weeks, you and your potential fiancé can decide whether you should consider marriage before accepting or making **a marriage proposal**. Something to notice is that the decision to move forward must be made by **mutual agreement**; if one of you **disagrees** with moving forward, **it is a NO-GO.** No-go is an old aerospace term for not launching or test-firing a rocket engine because it is unsafe to proceed. Therefore, you shut it down and figure out what the problem is before going forward.

If, after problem-solving, it is still a **No-Go**, you will stop courting that person and see who else is still within your friend group with whom you will ask permission to spend more time while keeping your single, non-exclusive status. Then, start the process like before and see what unfolds. If needed, expand your circle of friends to include other potential friends.

Sometimes, ending relationships after courting someone can be emotionally challenging. Resist the negative interpretation that you are a failure or someone's feelings will get hurt. Loving someone and having strong feelings for them does not mean you should marry them at all costs. Another perspective to consider is that some people struggle with trust or commitment issues.

Remember, love has three components: ***passion, trust, and commitment***. In many relationships, people who are wounded from past relationships have ***trust issues***, which can also present as insecurity. Next to ***trust*** is commitment, which will be difficult if you are in a relationship with someone with ***trust issues***, yourself included. An interesting article by Jeremy S. Nicholson discusses three reasons why people don't commit.

The three reasons are:

1. They are not satisfied.

2. They have other options.

3. They are not invested.

Nevertheless, if you realize you have passion, trust, and commitment after going through 10 weeks of premarital counseling, **feel free to move forward**. You may be ready to start looking at **rings** in anticipation of a marriage proposal.

Key concepts to remember during the courting stage

- Court one of your four friends with whom you have a plutonic or romantic interest.

- Remain in a *nonexclusive* relationship.

- *Ask permission* to spend more time with your special friend/romantic interest with the understanding that you have other friends you see but are not necessarily sleeping with.

- If the relationship is progressing mutually, ask them to attend **ten weeks of premarital counseling** to determine whether they should accept a proposal and pursue marriage with this person.

- No sex (if tempted, review the checklist on page 25)

- Choose wisely

- Don't ignore what you see. Character is important. The famous poet Mya Angelo said profoundly, "If someone shows you who they are, believe them."

Step 4
Engagement Stage 3

The goal of this stage is to move into an exclusive relationship with someone you have thoroughly vetted.

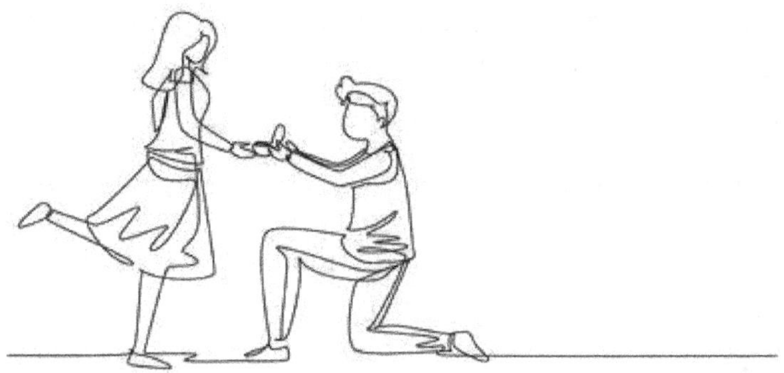

If it is appropriate in your family culture, seek the approval of the parents or surrogates of your fiancée before you are asked to accept or offer your fiancée's hand in marriage. Traditionally, this would be the father if they are living or an essential member of your fiancée's life.

Once you accept or make a marriage proposal that is accepted, you have entered into an ***Exclusive Relationship***. There will be much collaboration on selecting a wedding date and making wedding plans. There is nothing wrong with planning. Just do it realistically and collaboratively. Also, if you have waited this long to abstain from sex, it will be worth the wait to hold off until the honeymoon. However, the choice is yours.

Date setting can be challenging, but the sooner, the better. For some spouses, long periods between engagement and marriage can be stressful, depending on the circumstances causing the delay. *Empathy, patience, and healthy communication* will help one cope with the stress of planning a wedding and date setting. Also, if you or your fiancée cannot agree on when or where to have the wedding, this could be considered a **red flag** that may require additional counseling. If a date is not set within 12 months of the engagement, you may want to go to counseling or rethink your fiancé's commitment to go forward in marriage.

Lastly, once you move forward with the wedding plans**, avoid cohabitating** until you get married. I strongly recommend you do not cohabitate. The only reason you could consider **cohabitation is for *extenuating circumstances for a short period*.** If you want to live together and cannot wait until the wedding ceremony, urgently consider getting the marriage license and going to the justice of the peace or going before a judge or ordained minister and say **"I do."**

Research shows that couples who cohabitate for long periods of time divorce at a higher rate than those who don't. People who cohabitate for more extended periods and don't marry also have problems with trust and commitment. As mentioned earlier, Jeremy S. Nicholson's article "3 Reasons Why People Don't Commit" states that people who don't commit are unsatisfied, have other options, and are not invested in the relationship. On the other hand, those willing to commit appear to be satisfied, don't want to exercise different options and are invested.

Another thing you will learn in this stage is collaborative decision-making. You are now making decisions *as a couple and not as individuals.* You are going from a "**Me**" mentality to a "**We**" mentality.

In the engagement stage, you are no longer on the market as a single person, and your **new boundary** switches to being in an **exclusive relationship**. You are not sharing your **intimate time** or **your body** with someone else. In this stage, you should be smiling, laughing, playing, having fun with your best friend, and planning to embark on a journey for the rest of your life. You may also be nervous. If your anxiety gets out of control, consider personal counseling or seeing a doctor.

Key concepts to remember in the engagement stage

- You are in an **exclusive relationship** with plans for marriage and have set a marriage date.

- Discuss housing, banking, budgeting, life insurance, vocations, how soon to have children, where to spend holidays with family, etc.

Step 5
Marriage Stage 4

In this stage, the goal is marital harmony

Once you reach this stage, you enter into a lifelong relationship with your chosen mate. You have finally caught your prize match. The search is over. You are not alone anymore. By the grace of God, I hope and pray you have a healthy, happy, and long life with your spouse. Believe it or not, the relationship work continues.

I recall a story about a lady who bought a plant from a merchant. She took the plant home, and after several weeks, she noticed it was dying. So she returned it to the merchant, accused him of selling her a defective plant, and demanded her money back. The merchant asked her what you did to this plant. She responded nothing. He asked her, did you water it? She said no. He asked if he had given it some sunlight. She said. No. So the guy took the plant and gave her a refund. The merchant took the plant and gave it some water. Then, he placed it in a room where it could get sunlight. After a week or so, the plant came back to life.

You will need to give special attention and care to your marriage. If you neglect it, it will not blossom. Take care of each other. Continue to do what married couples do in a harmonious relationship. Have fun, play together, pray for each other, plan together, and actively listen to each other.

<h3 style="text-align:center">An important rule to remember</h3>

Don't let your **issues** become more important than your **relationship**. Issues will come and go, but the relationship has the most value. Cherish it. In this stage, you will spend your *lifetime learning* how to be married to your special person, so choose wisely. As part of your life learning, you must implement several practices to help you *transition from "ME" to "WE."*

<h3 style="text-align:center">Practices to maintain throughout your marriage life</h3>

1. **Be respectful, considerate, and kind to create a nurturing atmosphere at home.** You should also be committed to a healthy communication pattern. This pattern involves appropriate withdrawals, de-escalation, owning your negative self-talk, and regular validation of your spouse.

2. **Don't ignore reoccurring themes regarding gripes, frustrations, or discussions.** Recurring themes are like the check engine light on your automobile. The longer you ignore it, the worse it gets. Sometimes, reoccurring themes are expressed as a constant aggravation or unwelcome topic of discussion. When you notice a recurring theme, it is time to communicate the issue using a healthy pattern of communication. Practice active listening and conflict resolution skills. This will ensure that both of you feel heard and understood. If you still struggle to resolve the reoccurring theme, seek counseling.

3. **Practice healthy communication** One practice that impacts the atmosphere of the home is healthy communication. To have healthy communication, you must get rid of four things. In the book "Fighting for Your Marriage" Larson gives the following guidelines for healthy communication.

a. Use appropriate withdrawal/ask for a timeout when overwhelmed by an unplanned, uncomfortable conversation.

As human beings, we have moments when we are uncomfortable or can't engage in specific conversations. Often, a spouse may demand that the subject be dropped or ignored. Psychologically, when a person gets overwhelmed, they may become angry and have one of three fear responses: fight, flight, or freeze.

Acknowledge to your spouse that you need a **"time out"** and would like to revisit the conversation when they can be fully present.

b. Choose to Deescalate rather than Escalate

One thing you do not want to practice in your communication pattern is an escalation or going **"tip for tap"** to the point of yelling, cursing, and fussing. Rather than **escalate** into arguing, choose to **de-escalate** by injecting humor or stop talking about the activating event.

c. Own your Negative interpretation and seek clarification from your spouse.

Frequently, a spouse may negatively interpret what their spouse is doing or saying. Negative interpretation comes from negative self-talk. Negative interpretation can lead to ill feelings toward your spouse or other people. Just because you think something is true about what you have been saying to yourself does not mean it is true. Ask permission to share those thoughts with your spouse by acknowledging what you have been thinking. After you finish sharing your thoughts, ask a simple question: **"Am I right about what I have been saying to myself?"**

d. Validate each other rather than invalidate.

Speak well of and honor your spouse with your words. Affirming words are better than harsh words, belittling, or shaming.

4. Practice collaboration on significant decisions.

When it comes to decision-making as a couple, you need to decide ahead of time what types of decisions require collaboration. Discussion on an issue needing a wise decision does not imply that every decision-making issue must involve your spouse. Yet there will be times when you must communicate with your spouse what you plan on doing, which may impact them positively or negatively. Without collaboration on significant decisions, you are asking for trouble.

5. Practice mutual respect

Mutual respect guards the friendship and builds trust, love, commitment, and harmony. Putting your spouse in a place of honor is a good thing. Be careful not to cross boundaries or do things to disrespect, dishonor, embarrass, or shame your spouse.

6. Practice Love Languages

Something many couples need to remember is to **love your spouse the way they understand love, not necessarily the way you understand love**. Sometimes, the love languages are so close percentage-wise that it may require you to practice all five. Having to display all five love languages can be a bit taxing. But remember, you must work on nurturing your marriage. One practice that may make this easier is regularly dating your spouse to make the relationship exciting.

7. Practice self-care, guarding your mental, physical, and spiritual health.

You owe it to your spouse to take responsibility to stay in shape and healthy as much as possible. Letting yourself go and using excuses not to guard your health is an injustice to the relationship. If you struggle with anxiety or depression, seek counseling immediately. Hiding these struggles from your spouse is dishonest. Informing your spouse about your struggles is what friends do. If you are part of a faith community, cultivating your faith together is a good practice unless you differ on your spiritual worldview.

8. Practice being slow to anger and quick to forgive

In any relationship, the more time you spend together, the possibility of a disagreement or irritation could arise and wreak havoc in your relationship. One of the best things you can do is to **be patient, kind, gentle, and quick to pardon an offense.** When you choose to forgive or pardon your spouse, it does not mean they are not guilty of an offense; it means that you choose not to punish them and no longer have ill feelings toward them. Only offenses that are *deal breakers* will require deeper conversations and reconciliation. Holding grudges and not speaking to each other is unhealthy for the relationship. The biblical writer Paul says not to let the sun go down on your wrath (Ephesians 4:26). In other words, don't let a day go by before you guys are back in a harmonious relationship. Use your communication and conflict resolution skills to draw closer together. If you struggle with forgiveness, Lewis Smedes has a book entitled *"Forgive and Forget"* that can provide some guidance.

9. Practice growing as friends and have fun.

One thing friends do is check in with each other, pray for one another, laugh together, and have fun. Laughter is good for the soul and for the relationship.

10. Practice intimacy

In your marriage relationship with your best friend, one of the things you want to keep doing is working on intimacy. When I use the term **intimacy**, I am talking about creating **a safe container** within your communication where you, as a couple, feel free to talk about your ***fantasies, fears, and frustrations*** *without being afraid of being judged, shamed, belittled, or rejected.* However, these are the discussions to have ***before you say "I Do" and after you say "I Do."*** When a couple can talk about anything, it reduces the secrets in the relationship and creates greater acceptance, which can enhance sexual intimacy. A spouse can feel lonely when he or she cannot share thoughts and feelings with his or her spouse. Once you have secrets, it leads to mistrust and personal grief. One can find themselves present physically but absent emotionally or mentally.

11. Practice a healthy, monogamous sex life.

Unless you have sexual dysfunction or health issues, couples should enjoy healthy sexual experiences. It is essential to be sensitive to your spouse's sexual needs. Engaging in intimate conversations where you feel free to talk about anything can help guard your marriage from possible infidelity. For some people, these conversations could be uncomfortable, and if they are and you lack communication tools or are afraid, then seek help from a professional.

12. Practice caring about each other's feelings.

Lastly, be sensitive to each other's **feelings**. You should know your spouse well enough to know what hurts them or makes them happy. One way to continue to do this is to be an **active listener**.

Summary

Hopefully, the strategy and tools revealed in the book will help you make a smooth transition from **"Me "to "We."** You also recognize that you need to be prepared for a spouse-finding venture. One key thing to remember is ***not to waste your time or anyone else's time in pursuing a spouse***. Knowing yourself and loving yourself is essential preparation before you can honestly love someone else. However, know that one of the key strategies or thought processes to have is to ***manage your relationships; don't let the relationship manage you.***

In the ***dating stage***, you have been made aware of how your personality type could work for you or against you. As you venture out to make new friends, remember not to get into an ***exclusive relationship*** with a stranger too soon. Maintaining your autonomy is a great aspect of being single. Be bold and courageous with this stance because it helps you to ***vet*** people who may be pursuing you for the wrong reasons.

Once you enter the ***courting stage***, maintain those healthy boundaries and look beyond the surface of the person you are getting to know. Ask permission to spend more time with them without giving up your autonomy. Recall that unless you are engaged with the ring and a wedding date is set, you should ***stay on the market***. If you are not married, ***remain in a non-exclusive relationship***. Go meet the family and learn about their values and if it is a good fit for you. Remember, before you accept a proposal of marriage, attend at least ***ten weeks of premarital counseling with someone who uses Prepare-Enrich assessments.***

When you reach the ***engagement stage***, you are very close to making a lifetime choice. This is where all your communication and conflict resolution skills are a strength and not a weakness in your relationship. Remember to talk about anything that may be bothering you. Be on the lookout for unexpected trouble or temptation. You may be second-guessing your decision. This is a very vulnerable time. Your true friends or psychotherapists should be able to impart wisdom to help you process your anxiety. Remember, you are now in an ***exclusive relationship*** with the one you love. This stage is more like a betrothal. You can begin to look at this person as your spouse.

Once you are married, you will ***spend a lifetime learning how to be married to the person you have chosen***. The ***marriage stage*** is the most satisfying of the four stages of the intimate partner relationship. Up to this point, you have navigated all the stages, and now your new status is "**Married.**" The search is over. You have put in the preliminary work. Keep nurturing your relationship. As you grow together, connect with other couples who have been happily married for more than five years. Attend marriage retreats that meet your needs and enjoy the journey together.

References

- Adrienne Santos-Longhurst, July 12, 2023, Why Is Oxytocin Known as the 'Love Hormone'? https://www.healthline.com/health/love-hormone

- Chapman, Gary D. 2010. The Five Love Languages   Farmington Hills, MI

- Denworth, Lydia, Brain Waves Synchronize when People Interact, Scientific American, July 1, 2023

- Domestic Violence https://www.justice.gov/ovw/domestic-violence

- Fast Facts: HIV in the US by Race and Ethnicity https://www.cdc.gov/hiv/data-research/facts-stats/race-ethnicity.html

- Fredric Neuman, MD, Why Some People Can't Find Anyone to Marry? https://www.psychologytoday.com/us/blog/fighting-fear/201304/why-some-people-cant-find-anyone-to-marry?eml

- Gottman, John Mordechai and Nan. Silver (20000 The Seven Principles for Making Marriage Work. New York, Three Rivers Press

- Holy Bible: New American Standard Bible. 1995, 2020. LaHabra, CA: The Lockman Foundation.

- Hormones and transmitters produced during sexual activity, https://www.vinmec.com/eng/article/hormones-and-transmitters-produced-during-sexual-activity-en

- Intimate Partner, IGI Global Publishing House. (https://www.igi-global.com/dictionary/intimate-partner/82791#google_vignette).

- <u>Jeremy Nicholson M.S.W., Ph.D.</u> 3 Reasons Why We Don't Commit to Relationships <u>https://www.psychologytoday.com/us/blog/the-attraction-doctor/201506/3-reasons-why-we-dont-commit-to-relationships</u>
- Olson, D. H. and Olson (2000) PREPARE/ENRICH
- Revealing Divorce Statistics In 2024 Christy Bieber, J.D. <u>https://www.forbes.com/advisor/legal/divorce/divorce-statistics</u>
- Scott Stanley and Galena Rhoades, What's the plan? Cohabitation, Engagement, and Divorce. <u>https://ifstudies.org/reports/whats-the-plan-cohabitation/2023/executive-summary</u>
- Smedes, Lewis B. "Forgive and Forget" HarperCollins Publishers, 2007.
- The art of non-conformity <u>https://chrisguillebeau.com/to-stop-insanity-its-not-just-about-doing-things-differently</u>